THE BASILICA OF OUR LADY OF SORROWS

CHICAGO'S JOY: A Visual Tour

Friar Servants of Mary
The Servite Order • Founded 1233
Chicago, Illinois
www.servite.org

THE BASILICA OF OUR LADY OF SORROWS

CHICAGO'S JOY: A Visual Tour

FIRST EDITION

ISBN 978-0-9885563-0-0

Published by the Order of Friar Servants of Mary
3121 West Jackson Boulevard
Chicago, IL 60612

Editor-in-Chief: James Foerster, Communications Director
The Order of Friar Servants of Mary, USA Province

Designed and Produced by CUSTOM DIRECT

Principal Photography: John Shelves

Graphic Designer: Kristen K. Ohlhaber

Editor: Geoffrey M. Bevington

Printed in the United States of America.

INTRODUCTION

In 1956, when Pope Pius XII signed the declaration raising the church of Our Lady of Sorrows to the status of a minor basilica, he remarked to Fr. Roschini, OSM, the Servite Procurator General in Rome, "I want to honor the city of Chicago and Servants of Mary who have done so much to spread devotion to the Sorrowful Virgin."

From the 1874 founding of the parish on the outskirts of Chicago, to its elevation as a basilica and into the present day, Our Lady of Sorrows continues to honor the city and be a blessing to the Servites who established and continue to maintain it. In these pages, through word and picture, we tell the story of this magnificent building. Step by step, we present to you the extraordinary works of art in marble and plaster, wood and glass, paint and tile, which make up "Sorrows." As you take this visual tour, we ask you to please keep in mind also its unseen treasure: the people and ministries which have turned this structure of plaster and stone into a living, vibrant church for many generations.

Our Lady of Sorrows was not the first Servite foundation in the United States, nor will it be the last. It has become however, a symbol of the Servite presence in the city and our spiritual center. Although the costs to maintain such a building are burdensome, with the help of many whose lives have been touched by her in some way, we remain committed to preserving Sorrows for future generations.

Please enjoy this glimpse into the majestic splendor of the basilica. We hope that you are able to one day make a visit (or revisit) in person to experience the joy that is Our Lady of Sorrows.

In your dwelling place, O Lord of life, our eyes are filled with your beauty, our hearts are opened to your wisdom, and our minds are illumined with your goodness. (Servite Liturgy of the Hours)

Friar Servants of Mary

TABLE of CONTENTS

6-15   Inner Wonders - Basilica Interior ————— Chapter 1

16-27   An Introduction and Brief History ————— Chapter 2

28-33   What Defines a Basilica? ————— Chapter 3

34-37   The Sanctuary ————— Chapter 4

38-39   Our Lady of Sorrows Side Altar ————— Chapter 5

40-41   Seven Holy Founders Side Altar ————— Chapter 6

42   The 10 Side Chapels ————— Chapter 7

43-47   National Shrine of St. Peregrine Chapel ————— Chapter 8

48   Our Lady of Fatima Chapel ————— Chapter 9

49   The Purgatorial Chapel ————— Chapter 10

50   Sacred Heart of Jesus Chapel ————— Chapter 11

51-53   St. Juliana, OSM Chapel ————— Chapter 12

54-55   St. Philip Benizi, OSM Chapel ————— Chapter 13

56-57   St. Anne, Mother of Mary Chapel ————— Chapter 14

58   St. Therese of Lisieux Chapel ————— Chapter 15

59   St. Joseph, Father of Jesus Chapel ————— Chapter 16

60-61   Our Lady of Guadalupe and Volto Santo Chapel ——— Chapter 17

62-65   The Via Matris or Seven Sorrows of Mary Paintings —— Chapter 18

66-67   The Pieta ————— Chapter 19

68-71   The Choir Chapel and Reliquary Altar ————— Chapter 20

72-74   Lower Church Altar and The Perpetual Novena ——— Chapter 21

75   Conclusion

76   Acknowledgements

A VISUAL GUIDE TO THE BASILICA

Refer to this diagram as you navigate through the book. Each new location in the church will feature a thumbprint floorplan in the lower right corner of the page with the location highlighted.

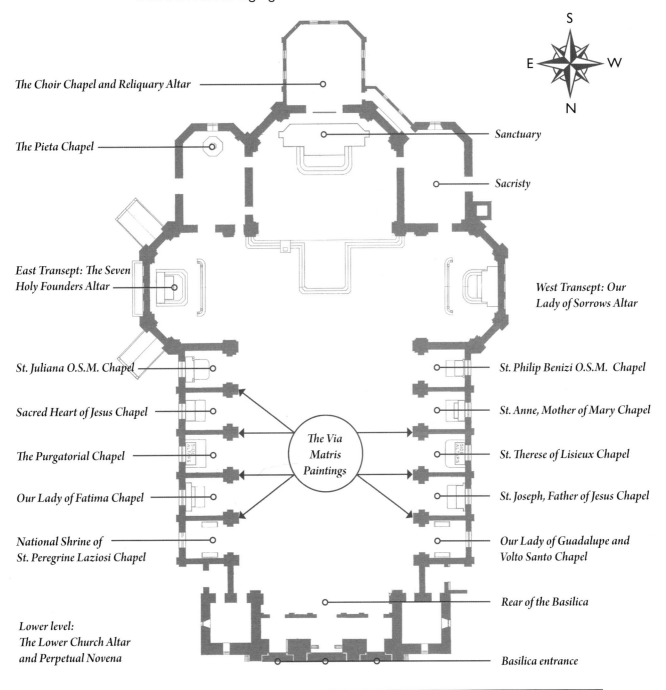

S

E — W

N

The Choir Chapel and Reliquary Altar

Sanctuary

The Pieta Chapel

Sacristy

East Transept: The Seven Holy Founders Altar

West Transept: Our Lady of Sorrows Altar

St. Juliana O.S.M. Chapel

St. Philip Benizi O.S.M. Chapel

Sacred Heart of Jesus Chapel

St. Anne, Mother of Mary Chapel

The Purgatorial Chapel

The Via Matris Paintings

St. Therese of Lisieux Chapel

Our Lady of Fatima Chapel

St. Joseph, Father of Jesus Chapel

National Shrine of St. Peregrine Laziosi Chapel

Our Lady of Guadalupe and Volto Santo Chapel

Rear of the Basilica

Lower level: The Lower Church Altar and Perpetual Novena

Basilica entrance

ALL ARE
WELCOME

Towering more than 200 feet above the artificial valley of the Eisenhower Expressway is the more than century-old shrine to the Mother of God, the Basilica of Our Lady of Sorrows.

Its massive, intersecting mountains of brown brick are topped here and there by dark metal crosses. A large bronze plaque, mounted on its masonry base, marks the elevation of the shrine to the status of a Basilica by Pope Pius XII in 1956.

In his words, *"This church is an outstanding place of devotion in America, where the Sorrowful Virgin is venerated. It is to be considered a powerhouse, whence heavenly works generate."*

With an open mind and humble heart, all are welcome to join the generations of pilgrims and tourists who have come before, to discover its beauty, history and traditions.

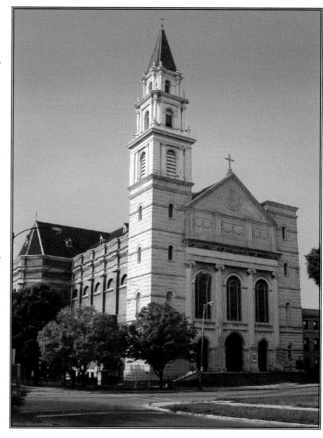

Exterior of Our Lady of Sorrows Basilica, present day

RIGHT: View into Basilica from entrance

ALL ARE WELCOME to the BASILICA of OUR LADY of SORROWS

ABOVE: Panorama view from entrance

THE INNER
WONDERS

The visual tour begins by passing though the heavy wooden outer doors into the small white marble vestibule. Pushing open the inner doors, which are covered with studded red leather, one enters the vast nave of the main church. Underfoot the pavement is entirely white marble and overhead, it is the color gold that dominates. Welcome to the Basilica of Our Lady of Sorrows.

LEFT: Entrance from Jackson Blvd.

BELOW: Ornate gold-leafed coffers

RIGHT: Interior view of barrel-vaulted ceiling

In a city with hundreds of churches, many of which are architectural jewels, only three have been raised to the status of basilica by Rome: the first, Our Lady of Sorrows (1956), Queen of All Saints (1962), and the most recent, St. Hyacinth (2003).

The Basilica Our Lady of Sorrows' Renaissance-style interior, modeled after the work of 15th-century Italian architect Donato Bramante, features a 75-foot high barrel-vaulted ceiling that spans 65 feet from pillar to pillar, consisting of more than 1,100 separate ornate, gold-leafed coffers.

ALL ARE WELCOME to the BASILICA of OUR LADY of SORROWS

LEFT: East-side chapels

RIGHT: Above the entryway is a painting by Michelangelo Bedini of St. Anthony Pucci being welcomed into heaven

The interior of the church is approximately 185 feet long, from the entrance of the church to the rear wall behind the main altar; 130 feet across at the transepts. High on the walls are semicircular clerestory windows, each containing a religious symbol relating to the subject matter of the 10 chapels which line the nave leading up to the main altar.

Replica of Michelangelo's Pieta

St. Juliana's Chapel

Marble flowers

Additional chapels in the basilica house relics of Servite saints and a full-size marble replica of Michelangelo's Pieta.

Beautifully carved white Carrera marble is featured throughout the basilica. Altars, railings, and statues display an intricacy and delicacy seemingly inconsistent with the cold hardness of the material. Stone flowers look almost life-like.

St. Juliana rests on a rolled pillow, which seems quite soft, until it is touched. Everywhere in view there are marble angels. They cling to the Communion rails and nestle in the high places. The church, as intended, is truly a tiny heaven on earth.

14　**ALL ARE WELCOME to the BASILICA of OUR LADY of SORROWS**

ABOVE: Panorama view from the Sanctuary to rear of Basilica

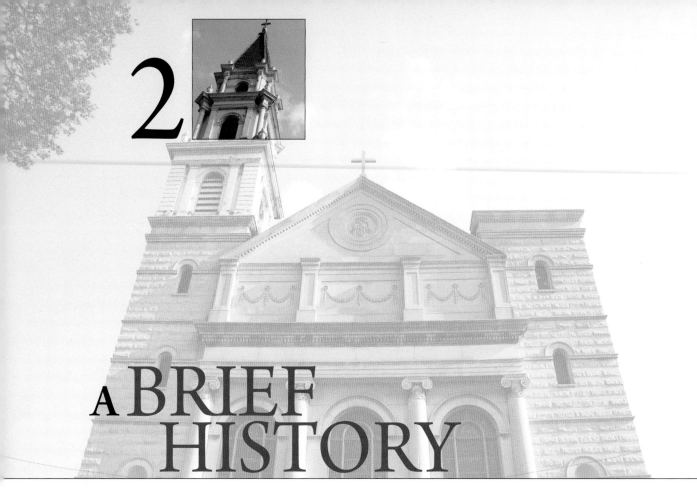

2

A BRIEF HISTORY

In celebration of the Diamond Jubilee for Our Lady of Sorrows in 1949, the Reverend George M. O'Connell, Order of Servants of Mary (O.S.M.), Prior of Our Lady of Sorrows monastery wrote:

> "Histories are often detailed; no one is thorough-going, complete. The attempt, in the following pages, to chronicle the first seventy-five years of the Church of Our Lady of Sorrows, the development of its inspiring plant, and to recall earlier years of renowned institutions that had their origin or major growth in "Sorrows" parish, is neither detailed nor deep-reaching.

Reverend George M. O'Connell, O.S.M.

> There is no mention of the master builders of Our Lady of Sorrows — the parishioners of yesterday and today — nor of the many and great sacrifices they made that their gathering place for the miracle of the Mass might be fittingly beautiful; their names are written in a book that will live forever…"

In this year, 2012, 110 years since the dedication of the church and 56 years since becoming a minor basilica, we stand in the shadows of so many who have come before us with a simple goal of sharing the enduring story of the Basilica Our Lady of Sorrows and the Order Friar Servants of Mary with a new generation.

Diamond Jubilee Program 1874-1949

The Basilica of Our Lady of Sorrows, present day

THE SERVANTS OF MARY

From 1874 when the parish was founded by Fr. Austin Morini, O.S.M., Fr. Andrew Venturi, O.S.M., and Bro. Joseph Camera, O.S.M., to the present pastor, Fr. Christopher Krymski, O.S.M., the priests and brothers who have guided the growth of the parish and continue to reside in the adjoining monastery have been Friar Servants of Mary, also known as the Servites.

Fr. Austin Morini, O.S.M.

Founded in 1233 by seven prosperous merchants who put aside their finery to live a penitential lifestyle, the group placed themselves under the protection of the Blessed Virgin Mary. Initially seeking a life of contemplation, the group established a hermitage on the summit of a nearby mountain called Monte Senario. Coming to be known as the "Friar Servants of Mary," others joined the first seven and as the group continued to grow, the seeds of the new religious Order took root. The Friar Servants of Mary were approved as a religious Order by the bishop of Florence sometime between the years 1240 and 1247. In the year 1304, the Order of Friar Servants of Mary received definitive approval as a religious Order in the Church by the Holy See. The Seven Holy Founders were canonized as a group in 1888.

Fr. Andrew Venturi, O.S.M.

Other saints of the Servite Order are honored and memorialized throughout the building. These include St. Philip Benizi, St. Juliana Falconieri, and St. Peregrine Laziosi, the patron saint of those suffering from cancer. St. Anthony Pucci, parish priest of a small Italian village is seen in a massively sized original painting by Michelangelo Bedini. This painting was used during St. Anthony's 1952 beatification ceremony in Rome and now fills the rear arch of the basilica.

Bro. Joseph Camera, O.S.M.

Three instances of ornate emblems of the Servants of Mary appearing throughout the basilica

Today, the Friar Servants of Mary, faithful to their tradition, remain committed to living the gospel in community and being of service to God and all people with Mary, Mother and Servant of the Lord as their abiding inspiration. A creative, apostolic force, the Servites extend their community to people of all ages, races, nationalities, and social position. Though always small in number, Servites can be found on every continent.

Painting of St. Anthony Pucci being welcomed into heaven

Detail from painting "St. Peregrine healed by Christ Crucified"
attributed to Gregorio Lazzarini (1655 – 1730)

THE
ARCHITECTURE

In 1874, a plot of farmland was acquired on Chicago's far West Side, and a brick church was built. It was 102 feet long, 38 feet wide, and two stories high. Midnight Mass was held inside on Christmas Eve, 1874. In the following year, the little church, on the site of today's Servite monastery, was beautifully frescoed.

Soon a much larger church was needed, and on June 17, 1890, ground was broken for the church we see today. The church was designed in the Italian Renaissance architectural style with various designs contributed by Julius Speyer, Henry Engelbert, John F. Pope, and William J. Brinkmann. The building was opened for Masses within months, under a temporary roof, while the walls had reached only half of their eventual height.

Original church built in 1874

PROPOSED
DESIGNS

One of the proposed designs by H. Engelbert

Design closest to the present day Basilica

PROPOSED CHURCH OF THE SERVITE FATHERS.

The most notable addition to the church architecture of Chicago will be the new Roman catholic church of the Servite fathers at Jackson street and Albany avenue. The accompanying picture is from the original plans, and gives a good idea of the general style of architecture, although some modifications have since been made in the details. Work on this new church is to be commenced in May.

The Servite fathers are a wealthy Italian catholic order, and are well known in America. They have mission churches in nearly every state of the union. In Chicago the home of the order has been on the site above mentioned, where the fathers have conducted a mission church for more than twenty years past. The new church, with its accompanying schools and residence for priests, will be the home of the order for the whole of America. The present church, which is on the corner of Jackson street and Troy avenue, is already too small for the parish. The latter numbers 500 families and is rapidly growing. The site upon which the new church is to be built is especially advantageous. It occupies the whole block bounded by Jackson and Van Buren streets and Albany and Troy avenues. It is 357 feet by 188 feet. When the new church is built the present church will be turned into a priests' residence.

French-Italian renaissance is the style of architecture employed in the new church, which will be a decided novelty in ecclesiastical architecture. The church will occupy a ground space of 272 by 145 feet on the south-west corner of Jackson street and Albany avenue. Two towers will rise to a height of 210 feet. The main entrance will be between these towers. The church proper will be 75 feet high in the interior. In the rear will be a transept, and over the intersection of the nave and transept will be an immense dome 75 feet in diameter, 260 feet high, and on the inside 180 feet in the clear. There will be seventeen altars in the interior of the church and the entire seating capacity will be about 2,500. The interior decorations will be very fine and costly.

When completed the new church will be one of the largest in America and also one of the handsomest edifices in the world. It will be the largest church edifice in Chicago or the west. About five years will probably be spent in construction and the total cost is estimated at $500,000. It is the intention of the Servite fathers to first construct the front portion of the building, which will be closed in temporarily and used for church purposes while the transept and dome are being built. The material used in construction will be stone, brick, and terra-cotta. The dome will be of skeleton iron-work with terra-cotta facings.

As a contrast to the usual Gothic style of church architecture in this country the new church of the Servite fathers will be attractive and novel. It follows closely upon the lines of modern church architecture in France and Italy. Julius Speyer, who is the architect of the new church, spent some time last year in Europe studying the models of ecclesiastical architecture in the old world.

The grand design of Julius Speyer (Chicago Daily News, March 1, 1890)

School House
68225

OUR LADY OF SORROW SCHOOL.
VAN BUREN cor ALBANY

Schoolhouse circa 1909

During the period from June 1895 through mid-1900 the transepts, sanctuary, basement chapel, side chapels and façade were added. The interior of the church, the work of W.J. Brinkman, was finished in December 1901, and the magnificent 1,200-seat church was finally dedicated in January of 1902.

On January 5, 1902, the church of Our Lady of Sorrows was dedicated as the Right Reverend Bishop Muldoun officiated and celebrated the church's first Pontifical Mass.

With the completion of the new church there began a new period of expansion and growth, the likes of which had rarely before been seen in a Chicago parish.

The new massive church sits adjacent to original 1874 church turned Monastery

RIGHT: Exterior of church circa 1910

A BRIEF HISTORY of the CHURCH

While improvements were made to the lower church, Fr. James M. Keane, O.S.M., was compiling a booklet of prayers to be used in a new service. This service, the Sorrowful Mother Novena, would take advantage of this new basement shrine.

On January 8, 1937, the Sorrowful Mother Novena began an era that would establish Chicago's Our Lady of Sorrows as a Marian Shrine of national and international fame. The great novena filled the upper and lower church with up to 38 separate services every Friday to accommodate the more than 70,000 people who attended each week. The Novena eventually spread to over 2,300 additional parishes at the peak of its popularity.

Perpetual Novena services were held in churches worldwide

Crowds waited hours for the next service

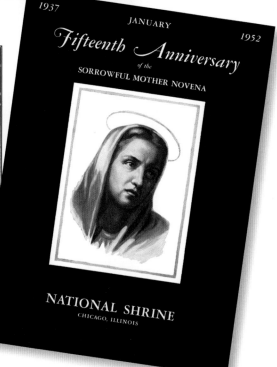

15th Anniversary Program commemorating the Sorrowful Mother Novena

A BRIEF HISTORY of the CHURCH

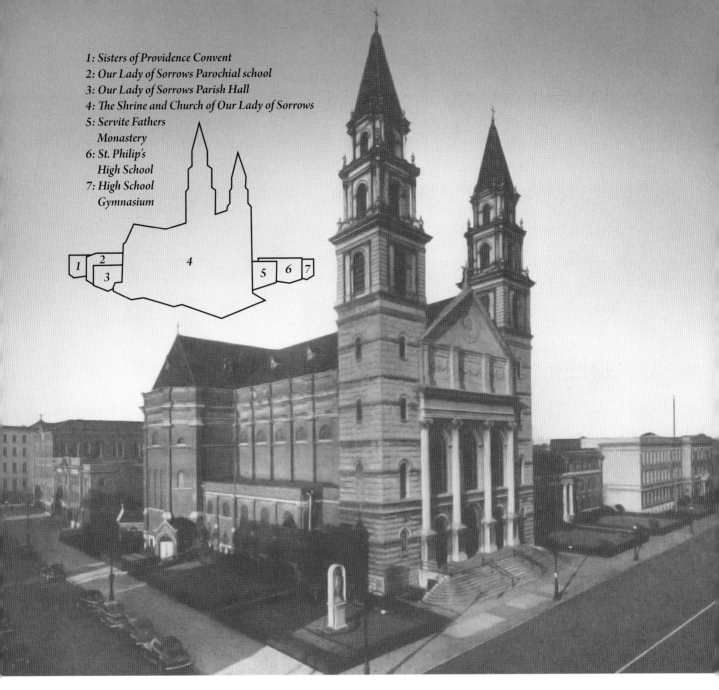

1: *Sisters of Providence Convent*
2: *Our Lady of Sorrows Parochial school*
3: *Our Lady of Sorrows Parish Hall*
4: *The Shrine and Church of Our Lady of Sorrows*
5: *Servite Fathers Monastery*
6: *St. Philip's High School*
7: *High School Gymnasium*

ABOVE: Basilica parish buildings line both West Jackson Boulevard and South Albany Avenue, circa 1949

By the 1950s, within the parish boundaries were located the church, the monastery, the grammar school and adjoining convent for the Sisters of Providence, two high schools with their respective gymnasiums, a football field, a residence for the Viatorian priests and brothers who taught at St. Philip High School, the parish hall, the provincial offices, and the Marillac Social Center run by the Daughters of Charity.

Serving these organizations were 133 religious priests, brothers and nuns, 55 Servites, 54 Sisters of Providence, 11 Viatoran priests, 10 Daughters of Charity, 3 Franciscan sisters, plus lay teachers, office and maintenance help, etc. Together, there were 242 people who served full time in some capacity during the 1950s.

The artistic beauty and the popularity of what had become the Our Lady of Sorrows National Shrine were factors in Pope Pius XII's decision to elevate the church to the status of a minor basilica in 1956. In honor of this recognition, a year of celebrations, the Coronation Year, was initiated on January 8, 1957, marked by liturgical celebrations and special pilgrimages.

RIGHT: Coronation Year program showing detail from the mural behind the Altar of the Seven Holy Founders located in the east transept (1957)

Dedication, Record Herald (1902)
"Interior of the Church of Our Lady of Sorrows, which was dedicated yesterday. The great beauty of the interior of the new Church of Our Lady of Sorrows marks it as one of the most notable architectural achievements in the West. The ceiling is of imposing height and is arched, the lines and curves being treated in an artistic manner. The altar is of great size and is made of marble. It is reached by broad steps. The large dimensions of the interior make it impressive. The acoustic properties, owing to the roundness of the ceiling, are excellent. There is an unusally large organ in the loft and also a big choir, which is heard to excellent advantage."

His Holiness Pope Pius XII

Within the larger Basilica of Our Lady of Sorrows National Shrine, there is a smaller shrine: the National Shrine of Saint Peregrine. Those who suffer from cancer and other diseases, along with their caregivers, are welcomed to a monthly Mass of healing and blessing of individuals with the relic of Saint Peregrine.

While the upper stages of the western tower were tragically lost to fire in 1984, the majestic east tower still stands over East Garfield Park and the Eisenhower Expressway. The interior of the church and the exterior brickwork have benefitted from periodic, and in some cases, ongoing restoration, in recent years resulting in a shrine that is breathtaking to many who enter for the first time.

St. Peregrine relic

CLOCKWISE FROM UPPER LEFT: Sanctuary lamp, stained glass window, votive candles

THE BASILICA OF OUR LADY OF SORROWS

In the past, Chicagoans referred to it as the church of Our Lady of Sorrows. Later, it was thought of as the Shrine of Our Lady of Sorrows. But, on May 4, 1956, Pope Pius XII erased all the old names in favor of a permanent title, raising the church to a new papal and universal status, forever to be known as the Basilica of Our Lady of Sorrows.

The Latin word "basilica" is of Greek origin meaning "kingly" or "royal." Basilicas were known to the western world long before Christ was born. In the Roman Empire, basilicas were courts of law. A basilica could be found in every forum throughout the Empire.

There are only four Major Basilicas and all are confined to the city of Rome – St. John Lateran, St. Peter, St. Paul Outside the Walls, and St. Mary Major. These four churches, or "Patriarchal Basilicas," are exclusively Papal: nobody may officiate on the main altar without written permission of the Holy Father. They are intended for the use of the reigning pope, they belong to the papacy, and in Rome are known as the Pope's churches.

PHOTO RIGHT:
Two of four paintings, known as the Basilica Tableaux.

CAPTION UNDER PAINTING:
On May 4th, 1956... Pope Pius XII personally signed the Papal Brief raising this church to the dignity of a Basilica Minor. January 8th, 1957, the 20th Anniversary of the Sorrowful Mother Novena...His Eminence Samuel Cardinal Stritch, Arch-Bishop of Chicago, presided at the solemn Coronation.

Canopeum

All other basilicas are "minor" and are considered part of the royal family of churches, or Arms of the Holy See throughout the world. Since it is a papal and universal honor, once granted no other authority can take it away.

Aside from the four great major basilicas in Rome, we associate the title of minor basilica with such world-renowned places as Lourdes, The Cathedral of Notre Dame in Paris, Guadalupe in Mexico, and St. Joseph's Oratory in Canada.

Other notable basilicas in the U.S. include: The Cathedral of Baltimore (Cradle of the American church), Our Lady of Perpetual Help in Boston, Our Lady of Victory in Lackawanna, N.Y. and the Misión San Francisco de Asís, also known as Mission Dolores, founded in 1776 and the oldest intact building in San Francisco.

In addition to the Basilica of Our Lady of Sorrows, Chicago is home to two other basilicas: Queen of All Saints (1962) and Saint Hyacinth (2003).

SYMBOLS OF A BASILICA
The external privileges of a minor basilica

USE OF THE CANOPEUM (UMBRELLA)

The most distinctive mark of a basilica is the display of the canopeum. It stands fourteen feet high and is constructed of alternating silk panels in the papal colors of red and gold. Its original purpose was to shield the pope and other dignitaries from the elements during outdoor processions. The canopeum in Our Lady of Sorrows Basilica is much larger than examples seen in other basilicas.

Constructed by the Assirelli Studios in Rome with wooden ribs and a special pulley to manipulate the opening and closing of the umbrella, the basilica canopeum was hand-sewn by expert seamstresses. Its lower multicolored panels depict symbols of the city of Chicago, the Servite Order, the coat of arms of Pope Pius XII, the Archdiocese of Chicago, Our Lady of Sorrows Basilica, and the Sorrowful Mother (representing the Novena). Because of its great size and weight (100 lbs), a special steel undercarriage was built, making it possible to easily wheel the canopeum in processions.

ABOVE: The basilica bell and the canopeum displayed in the Sanctuary

USE OF A SPECIAL BELL (TINTINNABULUM) ENCASED IN THE PAPAL COAT-OF-ARMS

The origin of the basilica bell is traced to the custom of ringing a bell to signal the coming and leaving of the Holy Father while visiting a basilica. The small bell, not more than six inches in diameter at its widest part, is mounted in an elaborate woodcarved framework and covered in gold leaf. From the woodcarving studios of Emil Thumn in Oberammergau, Germany, the reverse side features a carving of Our Lady of Sorrows, patroness of the basilica.

The bell is carried in processions immediately behind the cross bearer, followed by the canopeum. Today the canopeum and basilica bell are borne in procession not by the clergy but by members of the laity.

When not in processional use, both the basilica bell and the canopeum are displayed in the sanctuary. The right to these two insignias, being a pontifical concession, cannot be curtailed or abolished by diocesan custom or ordinance. From this use of the papal symbols, theoretically at least, a basilica is a church prepared to receive a visit from the Holy Father.

RIGHT TOP: Basilica bell (front)
RIGHT BOTTOM: Basilica bell (back)

FORMAL COAT-OF-ARMS

The special coat of arms, representing the Basilica of Our Lady of Sorrows is topped by the canopeum, the distinctive heraldic device symbolizing the papacy. Beneath the canopeum is a shield containing armorial bearings proper to the church, the Archdiocese, and the city of Chicago.

In the middle of the shield is the heart of Our Lady of Sorrows pierced by Seven Sorrows.

Rising from the Immaculate Heart of Mary is a rose symbolizing the Sorrowful Mother Novena, which in time augmented and spread throughout the world represented in the globe beneath the heart.

In the upper part of the shield is the monogram of the Order of Servants of Mary. This monogram is topped with a crown and seven lilies, indicative of the Seven Founders of the Order.

To the right of the Servite emblem is a phoenix, a mythical bird rising out of fire. The phoenix, a part of the coat of arms of the Archdiocese of Chicago, symbolizes the rise of the Catholic Church from the great Chicago fire of 1871.

To the left is a shield representing the U.S. and particularly Chicago. The sheaf of wheat on the shield represents plenty and industry. Above the shield, a half shell with a pearl inside — a symbol of Lake Michigan and Chicago — meaning pearl of the Great Lakes.

LEFT: Coat-of-Arms

Immaculate Heart of Mary   *Order of Servants of Mary monogram*   *Phoenix emblem*   *Shield representing Chicago and U.S.*

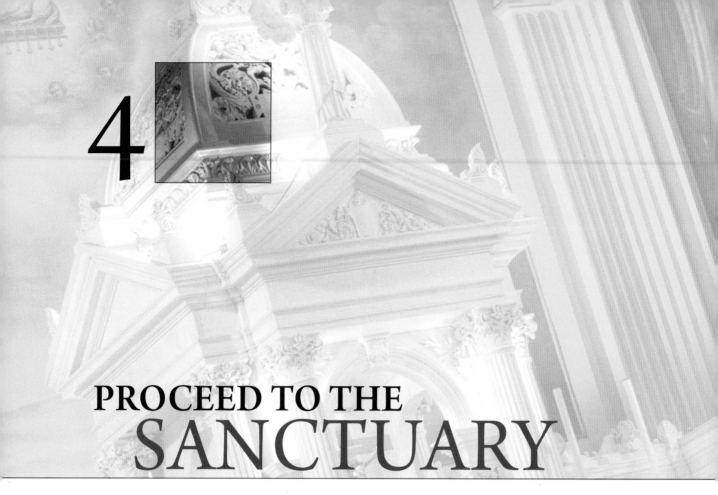

PROCEED TO THE
SANCTUARY

The high altar of Our Lady of Sorrows has been rightly described as a masterpiece in gleaming, white Carrera marble. Carefully proportioned to fit its setting in the vast space of the apse, its columns, pediments, and domes resemble a small temple and the structure captures attention from the moment one enters the church. A gift of the Altar Society, it was consecrated in 1908 by Archbishop Quigley.

The altar's role as the place of sacrifice is bolstered by the inclusion of three carved panels in deep relief: the sacrifice of Isaac, the Last Supper, the bread and wine offered by Melchizedek. Other carved decorations depict the Eucharistic symbols of wheat and grapes. Notice also the two round mosaics containing the intertwined M and S, the monogram of the Servite Order. Angels representing the virtues of faith, hope, and charity

RIGHT: The High Altar of "Sorrows"

stand atop the altar and along with the use of variegated marbles and gold mosaic work, further enhance the beauty of the structure.

The altar is flanked on either side by gilded balconies protruding from the choir lofts patterned after the balcony in the Sistine Chapel. The east loft contains the console of the 1902 Lyon & Healy four manual, fifty-seven rank pipe organ. The pipes themselves are contained in chambers located in both the east and west lofts.

Behind the altar are three large murals dating from 1917 and depicting Eucharistic and Servite themes. The painting to the east depicts the first Mass of St. Philip Benizi and is by Frank L. Giusti. The center painting, The Lamb of God in Glory, is also by Giusti. Finally, the painting to the west represents the communion of St. Juliana on her deathbed and is by Henry C. Balink. The paintings

ABOVE: Clockwise from upper left: Gilded balcony patterned after the Sistine Chapel balcony; The sedilia, or solid wood Priest's chair; Relief of the Last Supper

Servite Emblem, Priest's Chair

Brass Sanctuary Lamp

were the gift of Miss S. Fleming, Dr. L. J. Ryan, and the Morand family. The sedilia, or priest's chair, crafted of wood, stands on the baptistry side of the sanctuary. Its centerpiece is a Servite emblem, and the artistry of this throne-like chair brought praise from Pope Pius XII in his formal document raising the church to the rank of minor Basilica.

The great brass sanctuary lamp, shimmering with metallic passion flowers, burns day and night, signaling the presence of the Blessed Sacrament on the high altar. Made in Russia circa 1917 and designed in the Eastern Catholic style, the lamp was a gift in thanksgiving for the healing of a child by Fr. Tom Moreschini, O.S.M.

5

TO THE WEST
OUR LADY
of SORROWS Altar

A gift of the Fortune family and consecrated in 1914, the altar of Our Lady of Sorrows in the west transept is regarded as one of the finest small altars in the country. Similar to the high altar in materials – white Carrera and variegated marbles, gold and colored mosaic – its notable architectural features include a colonnade, central niche with arches and dome, and a statue of Our Lady of Sorrows. This is one of the most popular and widely visited sites in the basilica.

The altar railing, in matching carved marble, displays seven medallion reliefs depicting the Seven Sorrows of Mary.

On the surrounding walls, the two large murals of the Crucifixion and the Return from Calvary depict the desolation of Mary and were painted by Frank L. Giusti in 1917.

"Return from Calvary" by Frank L. Giusti

The Seven Sorrows of Mary Altar railing marble medallions

6

TO THE EAST
The Seven HOLY FOUNDERS Altar

The Shrine Altar of the Seven Holy Founders of the Servites dominates the east transept of the Basilica. A gift of John J. and Joanna O'Brien and Alice M. Powell, the altar was consecrated in 1931.

The Blessed Virgin Mary is presented in painted marble and Venetian mosaic, as she is said to have appeared to seven Florentine merchants, inviting them to become Servants of Mary.

Beneath Our Lady is a mosaic view of Monte Senario, near Florence, the first foundation and spiritual center of the Servite Order.

On the altar rail are seven bas-reliefs, each one depicting a moment in the life of the Seven Holy Founders.

A mural above this altar was painted by the artist Richard Schmid in celebration of the 1956 elevation of Our Lady of Sorrows to a basilica. The mural incorporates such diverse subjects as Pope Pius XII, the Vatican's Swiss Guards, Chicago's bustling industrial heart and its breathtaking skyline.

The mural on the north wall of this transept, also by Richard Schmid, shows Samuel Cardinal Stritch, Archbishop of Chicago, presenting the basilica proclamation in the sanctuary.

Both the east and west transepts contain their original confessionals of architecturally carved wood.

A Moment in the Life of One the Seven Holy Founders

RIGHT, MURAL LEFT OF ALTAR READS: "First and most important church in America dedicated to Our Lady of Sorrows... from this Shrine devotion to Our Sorrowful Mother spread everywhere like an inundating river... Pope Pius XII"

Samuel Cardinal Stritch, Archbishop of Chicago, presenting the basilica proclamation in the sanctuary

7

THE 10 SIDE CHAPELS

Turning from the high altar, we walk back toward the entrance looking up at a mural depicting the Glorification of St. Anthony Pucci, a 19th century Servite friar and pastor. From the rear of the church, the visual tour continues with a visit to each of the ten side chapels.

Each of the side chapels, nine with altars and one with a confessional, were added and embellished over time by loving and faithful parishioners. All have similar coffered ceilings, and many employ the single chapel window as a part of the altar piece.

BELOW: Mural of St. Anthony Pucci

8

St. PEREGRINE LAZIOSI SHRINE & CHAPEL

In 1283 Saint Philip, Prior General of the Friar Servants of Saint Mary, attempted to lead the citizens of Forli back to obedience to the Apostolic See. He was driven out of the city with insults and violence.

While this true follower of Christ was praying for his persecutors, one of the crowd, an eighteen year old by the name of Peregrine of the famous Laziosi family, repented and humbly asked Philip for forgiveness. The holy father received him with love. From that moment the young man began to scorn the vanities of the world and to pray most fervently to the Blessed Virgin, asking that she show him the way of salvation. A few years later, guided by the Virgin, he received the habit of Our Lady in the priory of Siena where he dedicated himself to her service. There, together with Blessed Francis of Siena, he committed himself totally to the Servite life.

After some years he was sent back to Forlì where, because of his love for God and Our Lady, he gave himself to the recitation of psalms, hymns and prayers, and to meditation on the law of God. On fire with love for others, he lavished a wealth of charity on the poor. It is said that he miraculously multiplied grain and wine during a severe shortage in his area.

Above all else, he was outstanding in his love for penance; in tears, he would reflect on the errors, which he thought he had made and would frequently confess to the priest. He afflicted his body with various forms of mortification: when tired he would support himself on a choir stall or a rock; when overcome by sleep, he preferred the bare earth to a bed. As a result of this type of life, at the age of sixty he suffered from varicose veins, which degenerated into cancer of the leg.

His condition deteriorated to the point that a physician, Paolo Salazio, who visited him in the priory, decided, with the consent of all the friars, to amputate the leg as soon as possible. The night before the operation Peregrine dragged himself before the crucifix in the chapter room. There he became drowsy and seemed to see Jesus descend from the cross to heal his leg. The following day, the doctor arrived to perform the amputation but could find no sign of the cancer, or even of a wound. He was so shocked that he spread the news of the miracle throughout the town. This only increased the people's veneration of Peregrine. The saint died of a fever about 1345 when he was almost eighty years old. An extraordinary number of people from the town and countryside honored him in death. Some of the sick who came were healed through his intercession.

His body rests in the Servite church of Forlì where it is greatly honored by the people. Pope Paul V declared him blessed in 1609 and Pope Benedict XIII canonized him in 1726.

A simple woodcarving of St. Peregrine Laziosi is displayed on the Reliquary Altar (page 70)

RIGHT: Stained glass window above the basilica entrance depicting St. Peregrine Laziosi

LEFT: Detail of stained glass

THE BASILICA OF OUR LADY OF SORROWS IS HOME TO THE NATIONAL SHRINE OF ST. PEREGRINE

Dedicated by Joseph Cardinal Bernardin on June 6, 1993, the shrine is located on the east side of the basilica near the main entrance, in the St. Peregrine chapel. This chapel originally held a confessional as did its counterpart on the other side of the church. The painted angels on the chapel walls, holding signs which speak of sin and forgiveness, reflect the chapel's original purpose.

While there are other artistic references to St. Peregrine in the Basilica, the centerpiece of the shrine is a masterful, seven-foot-high oil painting, "St. Peregrine Healed by Christ Crucified" attributed to 17th century Venetian master Gregorio Lazzarini. The Servites acquired the painting from the Christian Brothers of Manhattan College, New York City.

Near the painting is a Relic of St. Peregrine, patron saint of those suffering from cancer.

"St. Peregrine Healed by Christ Crucified"
attributed to Gregorio Lazzarini (1655 – 1730)

Relic of St. Peregrine

RIGHT: St. Peregrine Shrine and Side Chapel

SIDE CHAPEL 1

9

OUR LADY OF
FATIMA CHAPEL

The chapel of Our Lady of Fatima was originally dedicated to the Immaculate Conception. The beautiful, carved marble altar is accented with light blue mosaics, a theme repeated throughout the chapel. The chapel was a gift of the Young Ladies Sodality, and one can see their monogram (YSL) in the center of the exquisite tiled floor.

The statue of Our Lady of Fatima hovers above wood figures of the young Portuguese shepherds Francisco, Jacinta, and Lucia, the Fatima visionaries, and were carved by José Ferreria Thedim. The statues were blessed in Fatima, Portugal, the exact spot where the apparitions occurred.

The wooden sculptures originally formed part of a diorama in the lower church. The removal of this structure years later revealed a long-forgotten stained glass window, ironically, of the Immaculate Conception. This window is now installed in the sacristy.

SIDE CHAPEL 2

10 THE PURGATORIAL ALTAR CHAPEL

The Purgatorial chapel was erected in memory of Fr. Jerome Mulherin, O.S.M, by his friends. Fr. Mulherin was pastor of Our Lady of Sorrows from 1927 to 1929, and again from 1933 to 1937, the year of his death. A statue of the Sorrowful Mother in white marble surmounts the tabernacle. To the sides are reliefs of the holy souls awaiting release from purgatory. The altar itself is of black marble embellished with contrasting marble columns and blue mosaics.

Note also the tiled floor depicting stylized birds, most likely nightingales. Early Christians likened the cries of those in purgatory to the song of the nightingale.

Consecrated by Bishop Sheil on All Souls Day in 1940, the altar's inscription in silver mosaic reads "Beati mortui qui in Domino moriuntur," "Blessed are the dead who die in the Lord."

SIDE CHAPEL 3

11
SACRED HEART
of JESUS CHAPEL

The Sacred Heart chapel is one of many that uses the stained glass window as a part of the altarpiece. Erected by the Metzger family in memory of W.G. Metzger, the altar panels of white marble feature the Eucharistic symbols of wheat and grapes as well as the thorn-pierced Sacred Heart of Jesus. The statue of Jesus, with arms outstretched, is expressive of the deep love of Christ for all humanity.

This chapel also features a mosaic tile floor depicting a cross and crown of thorns. Unlike many of the other chapels, the wall paintings do not depict angels. Rather, here are images of the Lamb of God and the Pelican in her Piety. This medieval device depicts the pelican feeding her young with her own blood and was understood to symbolize charity and Christ's sacrificial love.

SIDE CHAPEL 4

12

St. JULIANA O.S.M., FOUNDRESS OF SERVITE SISTERS CHAPEL

The St. Juliana Falconieri chapel, the last of the east side chapels, was the gift of the Third Order of Servites (now called the Servite Secular Order) of which St. Juliana is patroness. The altarpiece is of Carrera marble, designed in Rome, and is the most elaborate and detailed of the side chapel altars. The recumbent figure below the altar represents the saint at the moment of death as she miraculously received Christ in the Eucharist.

RIGHT: Carrera Marble Depiction of St. Juliana at the Moment of her Death

SIDE CHAPEL 5

THE REREDOS

On the reredos, or back panel, of the altar is a reproduction in colored and raised relief of the miraculous painting of the Annunciation in the church of the Santissima Annunziata in Florence, Italy, the mother church of the Servite Order.

A reredos, or raredos is an altarpiece, a screen or decoration behind the altar in a church, usually depicting religious iconography or images. In French and sometimes in English, this is called a retable; in Spanish a retablo. It can be made of stone, wood, metal or ivory and the images can be carved, gilded and/or mosaic. Sometimes the reredos is a tapestry made of silk or velvet.

Annunciation in the church of the Santissima Annunziata in Florence, Italy

BELOW: Close-up of the reredos

The intricate mosaic floor tiles display the Servite monogram and a Latin inscription reading "To serve Mary is to reign." Notable also is the wall painting of an angel holding a sign which reads "Regula." This refers to the Rule of Life followed by the Servite Secular Order.

Convent, Omaha, NE

Schoolhouse, Cuves, France

Servite sisters, Ladysmith, WI

Treppio, Italy

The Order of Servants of Mary (Servites) was founded in 1233 on Monte Senario, outside of Florence, Italy. The Order is now worldwide and comprised of many autonomous congregations of priests, brothers, active and contemplative sisters, Secular Order members, Secular Institutes, the Lay Diakonia, and other associates, all sharing the same Servite spirituality.

SERVANTS OF MARY, LONDON/CUVES, IN OMAHA, NEBRASKA

The American Province of the Servants of Mary London/Cuves has its motherhouse at Our Lady of Sorrows Convent in Omaha, Nebraska. The history of these sisters is traced back to foundress Marie Guyot, the leader of a small group of teachers who came together in 1842 to educate girls in a small school in Cuves, France. In 1852, the sisters moved to London, England, to serve as missionaries teaching and caring for the poor. In England they became known as the Sisters of Compassion. They were aggregated to the Servite Order in 1864 and established a firm foundation in the States in 1892 at St. Matthew's Parish in Mount Vernon, Indiana. The sisters moved westward, establishing foundations in Illinois, Iowa, and Nebraska, and staff schools and ministries throughout the United States.

SERVANTS OF MARY, LADYSMITH, WI

The Ladysmith Servite Sisters were originally founded by five members of the Sister of St. Joseph of La Grange, IL, who left that community in response to a request for teachers made by the Servite friars at St. Mary's Parish School in Ladysmith, Wisconsin. They arrived in 1912. In 1913, the Mantellate Sisters Servants of Mary came from Italy to direct, instruct, and aggregate the early group into the traditional Marian spirit of the Servite Order. They were declared an independent diocesan congregation in 1919 and formally affiliated with the Servite Order in 1921. The sisters continue to respond to the changing needs of the times through a variety of ministries.

THE MANTELLATE SERVANTS OF MARY OF PISTOIA, IN BLUE ISLAND/PLAINFIELD, IL

The Mantellate Sisters trace their origin to the year 1861 in Treppio, Italy. The foundresses were two members of the Servite Third Order. Similar to the other sisters' groups, their initial charge was the education of girls and the care of the poor. The community was aggregated to the Order in 1868. They came to the United States in 1913 to instruct the Ladysmith Sisters in the ways of the Order. Later, they moved to the Chicago area in order to serve the immigrant population. Today, the sisters serve the needs of the Church in Italy, Spain, Africa and the United States giving witness to Gospel values in the fields of education, healthcare, pastoral work in parishes, and working among youth.

St. JULIANA FALCONIERI

13

St. PHILIP BENIZI, O.S.M. CHAPEL

St. Philip Benizi

Directly across the church from the St. Juliana chapel is the St. Philip Benizi chapel. Erected in honor of the great saint of the Servite Order, it was a gift of Mrs. Bridget Mulherin, the mother of Fr. Jerome Mulherin, O.S.M. The chapel was restored in memory of Philip Giancola, St. Philip High School Class of 1952, by his friends.

Graceful in line and proportion, this altar has beautifully carved panel decorations, a richly ornamented tabernacle, and mosaic monogram of the saint on the altar frontal. The decorated altar is surmounted by a statue of the humble saint in Servite habit with the papal tiara at his feet. According to legend, St. Philip was offered the papacy but humbly refused.

The chapel also has one of the most elaborate mosaic tile floors in the entire church. In roundels painted high on the chapel walls, angels are seen holding a papal tiara and crucifix, the traditional attributes of the saint also seen in the altar statue.

SIDE CHAPEL 6

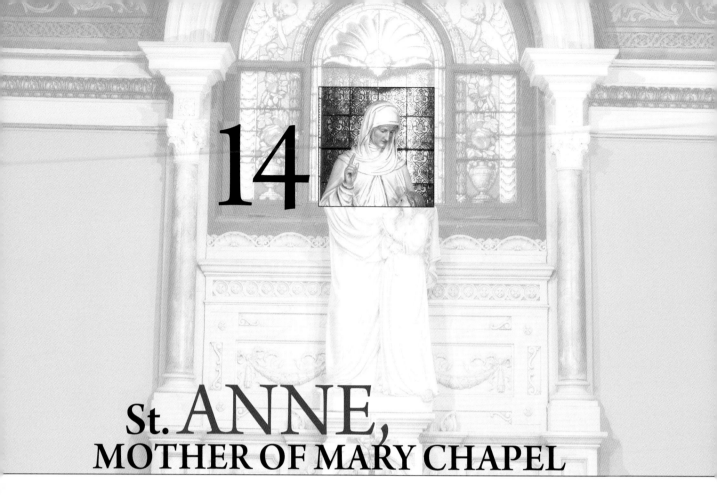

14

St. ANNE, MOTHER OF MARY CHAPEL

This chapel was the first of the ten side chapels in the basilica to be completed and contains the oldest altar in the building. The furnishing of the chapel was paid for by the Married Ladies Sodality which was formed in 1887 during the pastorate of Fr. Matthew McCann, O.S.M. It was also the first to employ the use of the stained glass window as a significant part of the altarpiece. Here, the window forms a "niche" in which stands the statue of St. Anne and her daughter Mary.

Cherub detail

Made of scagliola rather than marble, the altar features cherub and garland decorative motifs. The monogram of St. Anne, the intertwined S and A, appears on the altar frontal as well as in the marble railing at the entrance to the chapel. The floor of the chapel, similar to the St. Philip chapel next to it, has an ornately designed mosaic tile floor.

St. Anne's monogram featured on the altar

Scagliola (from the Italian scaglia, meaning "chips"), is a technique for producing stucco columns, sculptures, and other architectural elements that resemble inlays in marble and semi-precious stones. The Scagliola technique came into fashion in 17th-century Tuscany as an effective substitute for costly marble inlays and are exemplified by the pietra dura works created for the Medici family in Florence.

Scagliola's combination of materials and technique provides a complex texture, and richness of color not available in natural veined marbles.

15
St. THERESE OF LISIEUX CHAPEL

This chapel was completed in 1933 in memory of Dr. and Mrs. Edward L. Moorhead by Dr. Louis D. and Mrs. Moorhead. The major decorative motif here, appropriate for the saint called "The Little Flower," is roses. They are seen in the arms of the carved angels in the altarpiece, in the stained glass window, and in the colorful Venetian mosaic that accent the white and variegated marble of the altar. The saint's monogram, of gold mosaic inlaid in a shield of white marble, is located on the altar front.

Angels Holding Roses

SIDE CHAPEL 8

16 St. JOSEPH,
FATHER OF JESUS, CHAPEL

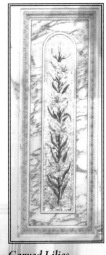

Carved Lilies

The St. Joseph chapel is unique among the other side chapels of the basilica in that its walls are covered in marble. The furnishings here were donated by the St. Joseph Sodality, comprised of the boys of the parish school under the direction of Fr. Vincent Healy, O.S.M.

If the rose was the dominant motif in the previous chapel, here it is the lily, the traditional attribute of St. Joseph dating back to Renaissance iconography. The altar is composed of white and veined marbles accented with gold and colored mosaic. An angel painted on the south wall of the chapel holds carpenter tools, symbolizing the traditional occupation of St. Joseph. On the north, the angel holds a sign reading "Ite ad Joseph," Go to Joseph.

SIDE CHAPEL 9

17 OUR LADY OF GUADALUPE
& VOLTO SANTO CHAPEL

Rather than an altar, this last chapel on the west side of the basilica still houses the confessional that reflects its original function. As it is no longer used for confessions, other devotional objects have been added over the years.

A statue of Our Lady of Guadalupe speaks to the years when the parish was primarily Latino. However, the object that arouses the interest of most visitors is the black and gold crucifix, the Volto Santo. This is a reproduction of the famous Volto Santo (Holy Face) of Lucca, Italy. The original thirteenth century crucifix was famous through medieval Europe and is mentioned in Dante's *Inferno*. The reproduction in this chapel was first displayed in the Servite church of St. Dominic in the Cabrini-Green area of Chicago and moved to the basilica when the parish was closed in 1970s.

Our Lady of Guadalupe

Volto Santo Crucifix

RIGHT: Our Lady of Guadalupe and Volto Santo Crucifix Chapel

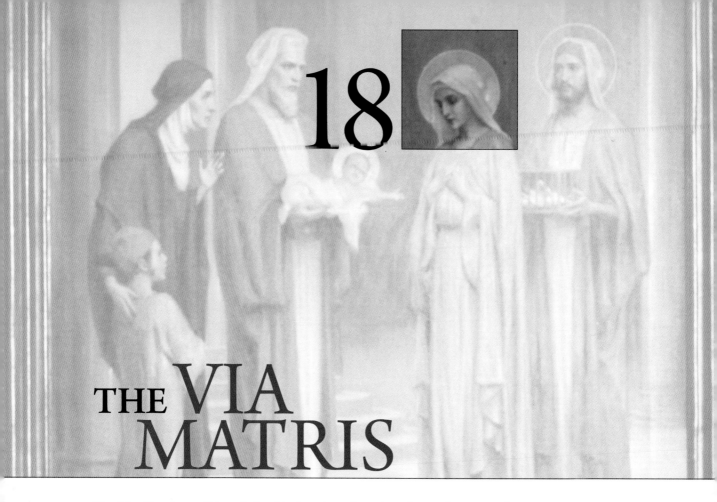

THE VIA MATRIS

The Via Matris, or Way of the Mother, is a devotion that reflects on the seven sorrows of the Virgin Mary. These seven events (also called the Seven Dolors) are frequent subjects in religious art.

Mounted on the pilasters between the side chapels are seven beautiful paintings of the Via Matris, done in 1939 by the artist Charles Bosseron Chambers (1882-1964). Bosseron was known for his portraits and figurative work, often with religious themes.

Chambers was born in St. Louis, and like many American artists at the turn of the century, studied art abroad, first at the Berlin Royal Academy, where he spent six years studying with Louis Schultz; later at the Royal Academy in Vienna with Alois Hrdliczka and with Johannes Schumacher in Dresden.

In 1916, Chambers returned to the States and settled into a studio at Carnegie Studios in New York City. Though little-known or remembered today, during his lifetime, Chambers produced extremely popular Catholic-themed paintings.

The Prophecy of Simeon. (Luke 2:34-35)

1

2

THE SEVEN SORROWS OF THE VIA MATRIS

1 The Prophecy of Simeon. (Luke 2:34-35)

2 The Flight into Egypt. (Matthew 2:13)

3 The Loss of the Child Jesus in the Temple. (Luke 2:43-45)

4 Mary Meets Jesus on the Way to Calvary.

5 Jesus Dies on the Cross. (John 19:25)

6 Mary Receives the Body of Jesus in Her Arms. (Matthew 27:57-59)

7 The Body of Jesus Is Placed in the Tomb. (John 19:40-42)

The VIA MATRIS

5

3

4

6

7

19

THE PIETA CHAPEL

The old baptistery is now the Pieta Chapel, home to an exact replica of Michelangelo's famous work and weighing 6,600 pounds. This chapel is a favorite of pilgrims and visitors to the basilica. Unlike the original work at St. Peter's in Rome, the sculpture is displayed low on a more human level and is approachable.

The Pieta was carved in Pietrasanta, Italy, by sculptor Spartaco Palla. Originally displayed in Chicago's Loop, it was installed in the lower Shrine church in 1937, and moved from the basement to its current location in June 1983.

A stained-glass window behind the Pieta portrays the baptism of Jesus by John the Baptist, a feature that harkens back to the chapel's original use.

Detail of the Pieta

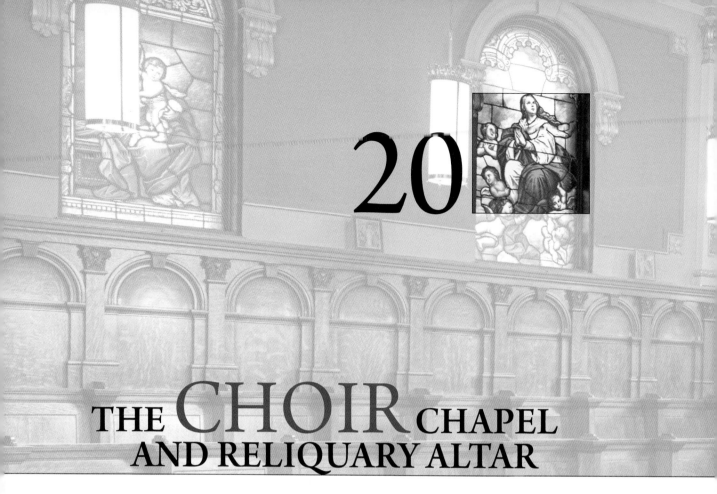

THE CHOIR CHAPEL AND RELIQUARY ALTAR

Directly behind the sanctuary is a small chapel. In the large European cathedrals, these are called Lady Chapels and dedicated to the Virgin Mary. This chapel was reserved for the recitation of the Divine Office (or Liturgy of the Hours) by the friars of the monastery. Completed in 1909, it is lined on three sides with two tiers of oaken choir stalls. Today, the daily parish Masses are held here.

ABOVE: The choir chapel at OLS

Mother of Sorrows

The Two Trinities

The Assumption

Six beautiful stained-glass windows by Max Guler of the Munich Studio were obtained from Presentation Church in Chicago and installed during a 1983 restoration. The windows are based on paintings by the Spanish Baroque artist Bartolomé Esteban Murillo.

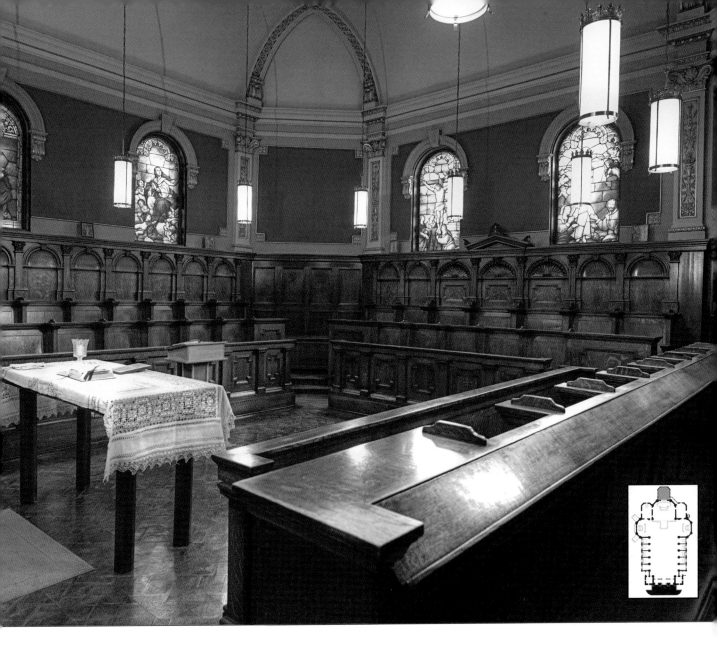

Crucifixion

Immaculate Conception

Madonna and Child

The CHOIR CHAPEL and RELIQUARY ALTAR   69

The choir stalls face a glass-fronted altar, a reliquary, containing over four hundred relics, some quite large, in brass containers of various shapes and sizes.

Above the altar rests a hand-carved wooden crucifix made in Mexico circa 1750.

Relic of St. Philip Benizi

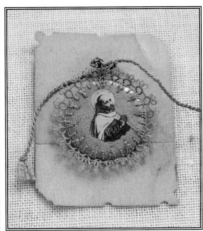

Relic of St. John of the Cross

Reliquary of St. Peregrine

Reliquary of St. Peregrine

Statue of Our Lady of Sorrows in the choir chapel

Statue of Our Lady of Perpetual Help in the sacristy

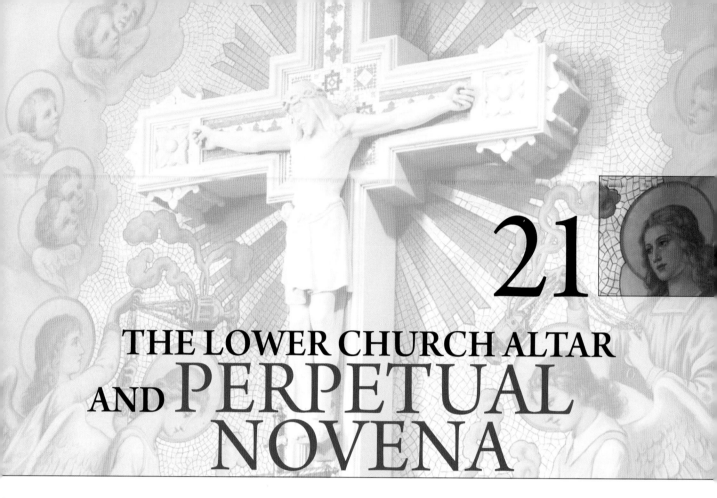

THE LOWER CHURCH ALTAR AND PERPETUAL NOVENA

For many years after the building's dedication, the basement remained largely unfinished except for a small grotto of St. Philip. In time, the grotto was replaced by a remodeled lower church designed by noted architect Henry Schlacks. The Servite Shrine Chapel, as it was then called, was dedicated in December 1936.

The Shrine Chapel's original decoration included paintings of the Via Matris along the nave (corresponding to the upper church side chapels), the Pieta statue in the west transept, and the Fatima grotto in the east transept. These are now located in the upper church. The high altar, called the Altar of Calvary and including a recumbent statue of the dead Christ, remains in its original placement.

The lower church now serves as the parish hall except for the sanctuary area which has been walled off to create a small museum highlighting the history of the basilica and Sorrowful Mother Novena.

THE SORROWFUL
MOTHER NOVENA

What was planned as a simple devotion on a Friday evening, January 8, 1937, the Sorrowful Mother Novena opened to an overflow crowd of more than 1,400. The following Friday, more than 5,000 faithful attended the services, a growing mass of Christians singing and praying "to Jesus through Mary."

At times, more than 70,000 people waited as long as three hours to attend one of the 38 services held in the lower and upper church and parish hall... a weekly attendance breaking all world records for one church, the first of many records the Novena was to establish in the ensuing years.

Fr. James Keane, O.S.M.

Their Chicago shrine could not contain them all, and their numbers filled the streets outside, spilling over into the cathedrals and churches around the world.

At its peak, the Sorrowful Mother Novena had spread to more than two thousand churches and convents in the USA and abroad. *Novena Notes*, known as "The Mighty Mite" among Catholic publications averaged a circulation of more than one million copies per month, while the Novena radio program, "An Hour with the Queen of Heaven" broadcast over Radio Station WCFL to thousands of the faithful every Friday night.

The Novena booklet has been translated into 31 languages and braille for the blind. To date, the Novena has reached millions and transformed the church, now Basilica, into a national shrine.

Crowds waiting hours in line for the next service

Fr. Clarence Brissette, O.S.M., at the live Friday night Novena broadcast on WCFL

Crowds fill the upper church

CONCLUSION

The history and treasures of a majestic building as old and vast as Our Lady of Sorrows Basilica are difficult to capture in a book's few pages. Text and pictures only say so much. Sacred spaces such as the basilica need to be experienced personally. It is hoped however that this book will serve either as a brief introduction for those unfamiliar or as a fond remembrance for those associated with "Sorrows." From a mere parish church on the Chicago prairie to its elevation as a basilica – the first such honored building in Chicago – Our Lady of Sorrows Basilica truly is Chicago's joy.

OUR LADY OF SORROWS BASILICA MASSES

Sunday Masses: 8:30 a.m. and 10:30 a.m.

Monday thru Friday, Mass: 8:30 a.m.

Saturday Mass: 11:00 a.m.

Holy Day Mass: 8:30 a.m.

For major Holidays, such as Christmas and New Year, schedule may vary. Please check the News & Special Events page at www.ols-chicago.org, or call 773.638.0159 for details.

THE BASILICA AND SHRINE ARE OPEN FOR VISITATION:

Monday thru Friday, 9 a.m. to 4:00 p.m.

Saturday, 9 a.m. to 12:00 Noon

Sunday, 7:30 a.m. to 12:00 Noon

If you find the parking area or front doors locked during these times, please ring at the monastery just west on Jackson Boulevard. Direct access through the monastery will allow you to tour the basilica at your own pace.

SAINT PEREGRINE HEALING MASS AND DEVOTIONS:

Third Saturday of the month at 11:00 a.m.

Second Saturday of the month at 11:00 a.m. (Spanish)

MUSEUM AND GIFT SHOP

A small museum and gift shop are open for organized tours upon request. Group tours can be arranged, highlighting the architecture or history of the shrine. We welcome weddings, school groups at all levels, and social organizations.

Contact: Shrine Director, Friar Servants of Mary

3121 W. Jackson Blvd.

Chicago IL 60612-2729

(773) 638-0159, ext. 102

email: olsparish@ols-chicago.org

www.ols-chicago.org

ACKNOWLEDGEMENTS

Many hands, heads and hearts went into the making of this book. To all those mentioned and unmentioned we wish to say a heartfelt, "Thank you." Of particular note are those whose insight and guidance helped to bring this project to fruition, including:

Fr. John Fontana, O.S.M., Prior Provincial

Fr. Conrad M. Borntrager, O.S.M., Province Archivist and Historian

Fr. Christopher Krymski, O.S.M., Pastor of Our Lady of Sorrows

Fr. Lawrence Choate, O.S.M., Friar Servants of Mary, Development Director

Drawing upon a wealth of information in the Province archives, we made use of several of the publications that have come before, including:

Our Lady of Sorrows 1874-1924

This 120 page illustrated history was published to commemorate the 50th anniversary of the parish.

Our Lady of Sorrows 1874-1949, Diamond Jubilee

This 80 page illustrated history repeats much of what is found in the 50th anniversary book and carries the story forward for another 25 years.

Basilica of Our Lady of Sorrows, Coronation Year 1957

Fr. Clarence M. Brissette, O.S.M., National Director of the Sorrowful Mother Novena, is the author of this 16 page illustrated booklet which tells the story of the parish and the Sorrowful Mother Novena. It served as a souvenir remembrance of the celebrations in 1957.

Basilica of Our Lady of Sorrows

This further update, an illustrated booklet of 14 pages, was printed about 1980 while Fr. Philip P. McGlynn, O.S.M., was pastor of Our Lady of Sorrows parish.

Photo Credits:

Page 16 basilica photo by Rick Grodek

Page 17 basilica photo by Diane Alexander White Photography